Journey to Freedom®

THE TUSKEGEE AIRMEN

BY SARAH E. DE CAPUA

"AS I LOOK BACK UPON MY LIFE, THERE WAS NOTHING THAT HAPPENED TO ME THAT EVEN APPROACHES THE EXPERIENCE I HAD WITH THE TUSKEGEE AIRMEN."
— BENJAMIN O. DAVIS JR. —

Cover and page 4 caption:
Tuskegee Airmen from the 99th
Fighter Squadron in 1944

Content Consultant:
Lisa Bratton, PhD
Assistant Professor, African
American Studies,
University of Maryland

Published in the United States of America by The Child's World®
1980 Lookout Drive, Mankato, MN 56003-1705
800-599-READ • www.childsworld.com

ACKNOWLEDGEMENTS

The Child's World®: Mary Berendes, Publishing Director

The Design Lab: Kathleen Petelinsek, Design; Gregory Lindholm, Page Production

Red Line Editorial: Holly Saari, Editorial Direction

PHOTOS

Cover and page 4: AP Images

Interior: AP Images, 5, 6, 8, 12, 14, 16, 24; Bettmann/Corbis, 9, 25, 27; Chip Somodevilla/Getty Images, 26; Corbis, 17, 18; The Design Lab, 20; Gabriel Benzur/Time & Life Pictures/Getty Images, 21, 23; Getty Images, 22; New York Times Co./Getty Images, 11

LIBRARY OF CONGRESS CATALOGING-IN-PUBLICATION DATA

De Capua, Sarah.

  The Tuskegee airmen / by Sarah E. De Capua.

    p. cm. — (Journey to freedom)

  Includes bibliographical references and index.

  ISBN 978-1-60253-138-3 (library bound : alk. paper)

 1. United States. Army Air Forces. Fighter Squadron, 99th—Juvenile literature. 2. World War, 1939–1945—Aerial operations, American. 3. World War, 1939–1945—Participation, African American—Juvenile literature. 4. United States. Army Air Forces—African Americans—History—Juvenile literature. I. Title.

  D790.26299th D4 2009

  940.54'4973—dc22

                    2008031939

CONTENTS

Chapter One

IN A TIME OF WAR, 5

Chapter Two

THE TUSKEGEE ARMY AIR FIELD, 9

Chapter Three

TRAINING AND DEPLOYMENT, 12

Chapter Four

PROVING THEMSELVES, 18

Chapter Five

HARD-WON RECOGNITION, 22

Chapter Six

A DOUBLE VICTORY, 25

Time Line, 28

Glossary, 30

Further Information, 31

Index, 32

Chapter One

IN A TIME OF WAR

hen World War I (1914–1918) ended, Germany was in turmoil. The country was on the losing side of the war, and had to pay damages to the winners. Germany needed a leader to improve the country. In 1933, Adolf Hitler became the ruler of Germany. Hitler and the **Nazis** wanted to make Germany into a large empire. By the late 1930s, Germany had taken over Austria and Czechoslovakia, and had begun to threaten Poland. Several nations realized the Nazi threat could spread through more of Europe. They began taking precautions against the Nazis. England and France began preparing for war.

One way these nations prepared for war was by building up their **armed forces** for combat on land, on the sea, and in the air. This involved making more tanks, ships, and planes. It also meant recruiting and training more men. The United States also built up its armed forces.

An important part of the U.S. armed forces was the U.S. Army Air Corps, a section of the U.S. Army. Any man in the country who wanted to be a **military** pilot had to apply to either the U.S. Army or the U.S. Navy. Pilots flew for both of these branches.

The U.S. Army Air Corps was closed to black pilots because the armed forces were **segregated**. But as U.S.

A group of men prepare for military service in Springfield, Ohio, in 1942.

entry into the war in Europe became more likely, blacks wanted to be able to join the armed forces as pilots.

By 1939, there were more than 100 black pilots in the United States. They had been flying in **aviation** shows and on long-distance flights. These men proved that blacks could be effective pilots. Even so, they could not serve in the armed forces.

In early 1941, the U.S. Army Air Corps announced that black men could finally become military pilots. The U.S. Department of War created the all-black 99th Pursuit **Squadron**. This was a group of fighter pilots. Fighter pilots had the most respected job in the military. They were known for their skill and bravery. Their duties included attacking enemy fighter planes that threatened U.S. bombers and destroying enemy targets on land and sea. Soon after the 99th Pursuit Squadron was created, an airfield was built near Tuskegee Institute in Tuskegee, Alabama, where the group would train. The airfield was called Tuskegee Army Air Field. The pilots who trained there became known as the Tuskegee Airmen.

The Tuskegee Airmen became well known and successful pilots in the armed forces. These men were the first black pilots in the military. From the Airmen's successes in World War II, the military finally realized that black and white soldiers were equal. This eventually led to the full **integration** of all armed forces.

In 1934, black pilots Charles Alfred Anderson and Albert E. Forsythe set out on their Pan-American Goodwill Flight. Their plane was called the Booker T. Washington *after the founder of the Tuskegee Institute. A major goal of the flight was to promote good relations between blacks and whites.*

The term "Tuskegee Airmen" most commonly refers to the black pilots who trained at the Tuskegee Army Air Field. However, the term also includes the maintenance crews and support staff who assisted the pilots.

Cadets training at Tuskegee
Army Air Field are inspected
by an officer in 1942.

A group of black men signing up for the U.S. Army Air Corps in 1941

Chapter Two

THE TUSKEGEE ARMY AIR FIELD

wo years before blacks were allowed to be military pilots, Congress passed the **Civilian** Pilot Training Act in 1939. This law established the Civilian Pilot Training Program (CPTP) at colleges and universities across the country. The goal of the program was to build up a force of civilian pilots who could serve as military pilots if the United States went to war. Training through the CPTP became available at a few black colleges, including Tuskegee Institute. At Tuskegee, the CPTP was a successful program. Every member of the CPTP training class received good grades, passed the flight test, and earned his pilot's license.

Finally in 1941, black pilots were allowed to train for the U.S. Army Air Corps. Tuskegee Institute was selected as the place for the military training base and airfield because of the school's excellent record in the CPTP. Shortly after, Tuskegee Army Air Field was built.

Tuskegee Army Air Field was a fully-operational training base. The base included offices and a headquarters. There were runways, living quarters, and mess halls where cadets and officers ate meals. A hospital, a theater, a store, and **hangars** were also built near the training base.

Tuskegee Institute and the airfield were located approximately six miles (ten km) from the town of Tuskegee, Alabama. Segregation and **discrimination** were a way of life in the South at that time. The town's restaurants and movie theaters had separate entrances and seating areas for black and white people. Water fountains and public restrooms were segregated, too. Signs that said "Whites Only" or "Colored" were common.

The townspeople did not welcome the pilot training program or the cadets. As a result, the black trainees depended on each other for support. The base offered sports teams, art exhibits, and other forms of entertainment. Cadets and officers rarely left the airfield grounds. When they did, they were harassed by white police officers and townspeople.

Many U.S. military leaders expected the program at Tuskegee to fail. Some considered it a test that would

Segregation and discrimination against blacks occurred not only in Tuskegee—it was common throughout the United States, especially in the South. Segregation continued until 1964 when the **Civil Rights** *Act was passed. The act outlawed segregation in restaurants, movie theaters, restrooms, and other places where segregation had been commonly practiced.*

show whether or not blacks had the ability, intelligence, and courage to be military pilots. The Tuskegee pilot trainees, however, were set on proving that they had the skills to become successful military pilots.

Around 1950, this movie theater had a separate entrance for blacks.

Chapter Three

TRAINING AND DEPLOYMENT

On July 19, 1941, the first class of black pilot trainees arrived at Tuskegee Army Air Field. Known as Class 42-C, it consisted of 12 cadets and one army officer. The cadets were all college graduates and included a police officer and a factory worker. The army officer was Captain Benjamin O. Davis Jr., a graduate of the U.S. Military Academy at West Point. He was the son of Benjamin O. Davis Sr., who was the first black general in the U.S. Army. Captain Davis had tried to become a military pilot in 1935, but he was unable to do so because he was black.

Training for Class 42-C began with Charles Alfred Anderson, who was the chief flight instructor at Tuskegee. Anderson had taught himself how to fly airplanes. He had not been allowed to take flying lessons because he was black. In July of 1933, Anderson became one of the first black pilots to complete round-trip flights in the United States. He brought his experience to the cadets he helped train.

Under the direction of Captain Noel Parrish, the training consisted of three parts: primary, basic, and advanced. Primary and basic training included ground school. In ground school, the cadets studied aviation science. They learned what made a plane fly, how weather affected a plane's flight, and how to read flight maps and **navigate**.

Advanced training consisted of military flying. The cadets learned how to change a plane's direction, speed, and height. They practiced takeoffs and landings. During advanced training, cadets flew with an instructor in the backseat.

Fighter-pilot training also included learning to strafe. Strafing means flying low and firing the plane's machine guns at ground targets. Pilots also learned to shoot at targets in the sky by firing at banners towed by other aircraft.

After eight hours of flight instruction, each cadet performed a solo flight. He took off, flew, and landed a plane by himself. On September 2, 1941, Benjamin O. Davis Jr. officially became the first black officer to fly solo in a U.S. Army Air Corps aircraft.

Noel Parrish was a white officer who strongly disliked racism and segregation. He believed in the Tuskegee Airmen's flying abilities. Parrish was one of few military officers who continually argued to allow the Tuskegee Airmen to fight in World War II.

Tuskegee cadets learning Morse code in 1942

In June of 1941, the U.S. Army Air Corps changed its name to the U.S. Army Air Force. In September of 1947, the U.S. Army Air Force became a separate branch of the military—the U.S. Air Force.

Five men from Class 42-C completed the training. On March 7, 1942, the five men marched onto the Tuskegee Army Air Field runway in a ceremony to mark the occasion. Lemuel Custis, Charles DeBow, George Roberts, and Mac Ross were made second lieutenants in the U.S. Army Air Force. (The U.S. Army Air Corps had become the U.S. Army Air Force in June of 1941.) Davis became a U.S. Army Air Force captain.

The five men became the first blacks in the U.S. Army Air Force. They also became the first Tuskegee Airmen. Other cadets soon followed. As each class graduated, the pilots were assigned to the 99th Pursuit Squadron.

In May of 1942, the 99th Pursuit Squadron was renamed the 99th Fighter Squadron. Also at this time, the 100th Fighter Squadron was established to get ready for the growing number of pilots who would graduate from the program. Lieutenant Ross was appointed commander of the 100th. Davis, who had advanced to the rank of lieutenant colonel, was made the commanding officer of the 99th.

Shortly before Class 42-C completed their training at Tuskegee, the United States entered World War II. On December 7, 1941, Japanese bombers attacked a naval base in Pearl Harbor, Hawaii. The next day, President Franklin Roosevelt declared war on Japan. By the spring of 1942, the first pilots of the 99th were ready for combat. The pilots waited for the orders that would send them to war against the **Axis powers**. During that time, the pilots continued to practice and perfect their flying skills. Months passed, but the Tuskegee pilots did not receive their orders.

By the end of 1942, Noel Parrish had grown tired of waiting for his pilots to receive their orders. He flew to Washington DC and met with Robert Leavitt, the Under Secretary of War for Air. Parrish strongly urged Leavitt to send the Tuskegee pilots overseas to contribute to the war effort. He knew they were prepared for the challenge.

In early 1943, Secretary of War Henry Stimson visited Tuskegee Army Air Field. Stimson was one

The U.S. Army has different levels of soldiers. Here is a shortened list of rankings from highest position to lowest.
General
Colonel
Major
Captain
Lieutenant
Sergeant
Corporal
Private

This U.S. Navy battleship was destroyed by the Japanese attack at Pearl Harbor, Hawaii, on December 7, 1941.

of the military officials who had been opposed to black pilots in combat. After his visit, he realized the Tuskegee Airmen were fit and able to serve their country. He described them as "outstanding by any standard."

Finally, on April 1, 1943, the 400 members of the 99th Fighter Squadron received their orders for **deployment**. They boarded a troop ship that took them across the Atlantic Ocean to the war in North Africa and Europe. Before they left, Colonel Parrish reminded the pilots that their future depended "on how determined you are not to give satisfaction to those who would like to see you fail."

The first graduating class of Tuskegee Airmen pilots and an instructor (center) on March 7, 1942

Tuskegee Airmen pilots kneeling before a P-51 airplane while stationed in Italy in 1944

Chapter Four

PROVING THEMSELVES

he 99th Fighter Squadron played an important role on the ship that brought them to North Africa. Lieutenant Colonel Davis was the officer in charge of the 3,900 troops while on board. The 99th was in charge of daily activities and schedules. The men thought they might now be part of an integrated army. On the ship, it seemed racial discrimination was not as widespread as it was at home. The 99th hoped this would continue once the ship docked. But the Tuskegee Airmen found that discrimination still happened.

The 99th arrived at Casablanca, Morocco, in April of 1943. The pilots trained in Morocco for one month in P-40 Warhawk airplanes.

After training, the 99th moved to a combat base in Tunisia. Their duties included guiding bombers and ship **convoys** and protecting them from enemy fighter planes. The 99th also strafed enemy targets, such as bridges and truck convoys.

In June of 1943, the pilots of the 99th experienced their first combat. They were leading bombers to the Italian island of Pantelleria when a group of German fighter planes engaged them in combat. All the planes of the 99th returned safely to base. During the fight, the squadron scored its first aerial victory when Lieutenant Hall shot down a German fighter plane.

The 99th moved from North Africa to the southern coast of Sicily, an Italian island in the Mediterranean Sea. Throughout July and August, the squadron helped U.S. troops advance through Sicily.

In spite of the fine work and fighting ability shown by black pilots, army leaders continued to oppose the squadron's involvement in the war. Colonel William Momyer was the commander of the 33rd Fighter Group. This was a white squadron to which the 99th was joined. Momyer told U.S. Army leaders that the 99th was not as good as the other fighter squadrons. When word got out, *Time* magazine featured an article that suggested top air commanders were about to remove the 99th from combat duty.

These rumors upset Colonel Benjamin O. Davis Jr. He had returned to the United States to command the

Benjamin O. Davis Jr. excelled in the military. After World War II, he became the first black general in the U.S. Air Force. He was a commanding officer during the Vietnam War. In 1998, President Clinton made Davis a four-star general. Davis died in 2002.

Key Tuskegee missions

Tuskegee training base

Tuskegee combat base

Allied countries

Germany 1942–1945

Associated with Germany

Neutral countries

GERMANY

SWITZ.

HUNGARY

FRANCE

YUGOSLAVIA

ITALY

CORSICA

Cassino
Nov. 1943–May 1944

Rome-Arno
Jan.–Sept. 1944

PORTUGAL

SPAIN

SARDINIA

Anzio
Jan. 1944

Naples-Foggia
Sept. 1943–Jan. 1944

SICILY

Mediterranean Sea

Invasion of Sicily
July–Aug. of 1943

SPANISH MOROCCO

ALGERIA

TUNISIA

Pantelleria
June 1943

MOROCCO

Casablanca

AFRICA

During World War II, the
Tuskegee Airmen trained
in northern Africa and flew
successful missions in Italy.

332nd Fighter Group, another black squadron. He spoke before a U.S. Department of War committee to defend the abilities and combat record of the 99th pilots.

In reaction to this debate, Army Chief of Staff General George Marshall ordered a review to determine how skilled the pilots truly were. The review showed the 99th was equal to—if not *better* than—white squadrons with similar experience in the war zone.

Benjamin O. Davis Jr. at flight-training school in 1942

Chapter Five

HARD-WON RECOGNITION

In January of 1944, the 99th Fighter Squadron began protecting the invasion of Anzio, Italy, by the **Allied powers**. The squadron first fought a group of German fighters. Five enemy planes were shot down. Later that month, three more enemy planes were destroyed. One 99th pilot was killed.

The squadron began receiving praise for its achievements. News of the 99th's victories was carried in newspapers, on the radio, and in **newsreels** throughout the nation. U.S. Army Air Force leaders who had expected the 99th to fail finally accepted that the pilots had earned a place of honor in the war.

In February of 1944, Colonel Davis returned to the war with the 332nd Fighter Group. In June, Davis's men were assigned to protect, or escort, the crews of bombers on missions to enemy territory. The 332nd Fighter Group's protection allowed the bombers to destroy German bunkers and airfields on the ground. Davis's men flew P-51s, the best fighter planes in the U.S. Army Air Force. The men painted the tails of their planes red, earning the nickname the Red Tails.

The U.S. Army Air Force bombers welcomed the Red Tails. Bomber crews admired the pilots' skills. The squadron had a near-perfect record. Few bombers were shot down when Red Tail pilots were with them.

One reason the Red Tail pilots painted their planes' tails red was to distinguish themselves from other fighter groups. They wanted to be memorable—and they were. Soon, the Red Tails were the most requested escort group because of their unmatched success in the air.

Benjamin O. Davis Jr. (left) inspected his cadets at flight training school.

The Distinguished Flying Cross is a medal awarded to those showing heroism or extraordinary achievement while flying an aircraft. The Bronze Star is a medal awarded for heroic service or achievement that does not involve flying an aircraft. The Purple Heart is a medal awarded to members of the armed forces who are wounded or killed in action.

The pilots of the 332nd were rewarded for their excellent combat record. The honors they received included 95 Distinguished Flying Crosses, 14 Bronze Stars, and 8 Purple Hearts.

No escort group's record equaled that of the Red Tails and other Tuskegee Airmen. When training ended at Tuskegee Army Air Field in 1946, 992 pilots had graduated and 450 had been sent overseas to contribute to World War II.

A U.S. Army Air Force pilot flying a P-51, the same plane flown by the 332nd Fighter Group

Mayor Fiorella LaGuardia (front, center) of New York City congratulated Tuskegee Airmen pilots in 1943.

Chapter Six

A DOUBLE VICTORY

fter World War II ended, the Tuskegee Airmen returned to a segregated United States. A life of segregation at home was difficult for them to accept after experiencing integration in the army. Even with their outstanding war records, the black pilots were treated as second-class citizens once they were back home. During the war, the pilots were determined to win a victory over the Axis powers. After returning to the United States, many became determined to win a victory over segregation and discrimination as well.

Once the war ended, military officials needed to decide what role black troops would play in the armed forces. Colonel Parrish, the white training

Former Secretary of State and U.S. Army General Colin Powell spoke during the Congressional Gold Medal Ceremony for the Tuskegee Airmen in 2007.

In 1942, one of the largest black newspapers in the United States, the Pittsburgh Courier, *started the "Double V" campaign. The "Double V" stood for victory abroad against the Axis powers and victory at home against segregation. The campaign pointed out the unfairness of black soldiers facing discrimination in the United States after risking their lives to defend the country in World War II.*

officer at Tuskegee, called for full integration of the military. He stated that discriminating against blacks in the military was unconstitutional. Parrish said blacks were citizens just as much as whites, so black troops deserved equal treatment under the law. Several other officers, both white and black, continued to argue for full integration in all armed forces.

In July of 1948, President Harry S. Truman issued Executive Order 9981. This led to the integration of all U.S. armed forces. The order required equal treatment of soldiers, regardless of race.

The Tuskegee Airmen's contributions to the civil rights movement were important. These pilots proved that blacks could successfully serve their country. Due in large part to their efforts and skills, the armed forces integrated. Military integration sparked the beginning of other integration in the United States.

Since the Tuskegee Airmen, countless black soldiers and pilots have made outstanding contributions to military service. Many lesser-known servicemen in the Korean, Vietnam, and Persian Gulf wars carried on the legacy of the Tuskegee Airmen. Cadets currently training at the U.S. military's service academies continue the Airmen's legacy in modern times.

Today, the Tuskegee Airmen exist as a **nonprofit** organization. The goals of Tuskegee Airmen, Inc. include honoring the pilots of World War II and introducing aviation to the next generations. Every year, former pilots gather at the Tuskegee Airmen Convention. Recently, a U.S. Air Force general spoke to the men who opened the doors for future black pilots. He thanked them for being "the giants onto whose shoulders I climbed to achieve."

In 2007, Congress awarded the Congressional Medal of Honor to all Tuskegee Airmen. The medal is the highest civilian award given by Congress. It was awarded in honor of the Tuskegee Airmen's contributions during World War II.

Tuskegee Airmen stationed in Italy in 1944.

TIME LINE

1880   **1930**   **1940**

1881
Booker T. Washington founds the Tuskegee Institute near Tuskegee, Alabama.

1933
Charles Alfred Anderson and Albert E. Forsythe make several long-distance and transcontinental flights.

1939
Congress passes the Civilian Pilot Training Act. More than 100 black pilots are licensed in the United States.

1941
The U.S. Army Air Corps permits the training of black pilots and establishes the 99th Pursuit Squadron. Class 42-C arrives at Tuskegee Institute on July 19.

1941
On December 7, the Japanese attack Pearl Harbor, Hawaii, drawing the United States into World War II.

1942
The first class of Tuskegee Airmen pilots graduate on March 7, becoming the first official black pilots in the U.S. Army Air Force.

1943
The 99th Fighter Squadron joins the war effort in Europe.

1944
The Red Tails, members of the 332nd Fighter Group, distinguish themselves on bomber escort missions.

1945
The Red Tails fly their final mission on April 30. World War II ends on September 2.

1946
Training at Tuskegee Army Air Field ends.

1947
The U.S. Air Force becomes a separate branch of the military.

1948
President Harry S. Truman issues Executive Order 9981, which leads to the integration of all U.S. armed forces.

1959
Former Tuskegee Airman Benjamin O. Davis Jr. becomes the first black general in the U.S. Air Force.

2007
Congress awards the Tuskegee Airmen with the Congressional Medal of Honor for their contributions to World War II.

Glossary

Allied powers
(*al*-eyed **pow**-urz)
The Allied powers were the countries of the United States, Great Britain, and the Soviet Union, which fought against the Axis powers during World War II. The Tuskegee Airmen fought for the Allied powers.

armed forces
(*armd fors*-ez)
All branches of a military, including the army, navy, and air force, that protect a nation. The success of the Tuskegee Airmen eventually led to racial integration within all U.S. armed forces.

aviation
(*ay-vee-**ay**-shun*)
Aviation means related to flying an airplane. Before black pilots could be in the armed forces, they were in aviation shows.

Axis powers
(*ak-siss **pow**-urz*)
The Axis powers were the countries of Germany, Italy, and Japan, which fought against the Allied powers during World War II. The Tuskegee Airmen fought against fighter pilots from the Axis powers.

cadets
(*kuh-**dets***)
Cadets are people who are training to become members of the armed forces. The first class at Tuskegee had 12 cadets.

civilian
(*sih-**vil**-yun*)
A civilian is anyone who is not in the armed forces. The Civilian Pilot Training Program built up a force of civilian pilots who could serve in the military in a time of war.

civil rights
(*siv-il **rites***)
Civil rights are personal freedoms that belong to all citizens. After the war, Tuskegee Airmen fought for black people's civil rights in the United States.

convoys
(*kon-voyz*)
Convoys are groups of ships, military vehicles, or trucks that travel together. The 99th Fighter Squadron flew above convoys of ships to protect them from being attacked by German fighter planes.

deployment
(*de-**ploy**-munt*)
A deployment is when troops are brought into military action. The deployment of the Tuskegee Airmen came after months of waiting to fly in the war.

discrimination
(*diss-krim-i-**nay**-shun*)
Discrimination is unfair treatment of people based on differences of race, gender, religion, or culture. Black people faced discrimination in the armed forces.

hangars
(*hang*-urz)
Hangars are buildings that store airplanes. Tuskegee Army Air Field had hangars on the base.

integration
(*in-tuh-**gray**-shun*)
Integration is the act of allowing different race, class, or ethnic groups to be together in public facilities. The Tuskegee Airmen pilots played a key role in the integration of the armed forces.

military
(*mil-uh-tayr-ee*)
Military is something that relates to a country's armed forces. The Tuskegee Airmen were military pilots in World War II.

navigate
(*nav-uh-gayt*)
Guiding an aircraft or other vehicle using maps and instruments is to navigate. During training, the Tuskegee Airmen learned how to properly navigate their aircrafts.

Nazis
(*not*-seez)
The Nazis were a group who tried to rid the society of what they thought were "impure" races during World War II. Adolf Hitler was the leader of the Nazis.

newsreels
(*nooz*-reelz)
Newsreels are short movies about current events that were shown in movie theaters. United States citizens learned about World War II by watching newsreels.

nonprofit
(*non-**prof**-it*)
A nonprofit organization is a group that does not make money. Tuskegee Airmen, Inc. is a nonprofit organization.

segregated
(*seg-ruh-gay-tuhd*)
When race, class, or ethnic groups are kept apart, they are segregated. The armed forces were segregated when the Tuskegee Airmen first joined the war effort.

squadron
(*skwahd-run*)
A squadron is a group of troops and their machines. The 99th Fighter Squadron consisted of black pilots and their aircraft.

Further Information

Books

Clinton, Catherine. *The Black Soldier: 1492 to Present*. New York: Houghton Mifflin, 2000.

Fleischman, John. *Black and White Airmen: Their True History*. New York: Houghton Mifflin, 2007.

Hasday, Judy L. *The Civil Rights Act of 1964: An End to Racial Segregation*. New York: Chelsea House, 2007.

Johnson, Angela. *Wind Flyers*. New York: Simon & Schuster, 2007.

Jones, Steven L. *The Red Tails: World War II's Tuskegee Airmen*. Logan, IA: Perfection Learning, 2002.

Sharp, Anne Wallace. *Dream Deferred: The Jim Crow Era*. New York: Gale, 2005.

Videos

Flying for Freedom: Untold Stories of the Tuskegee Airmen. Dir. Tom Rubeck. AMS, 2007.

The Tuskegee Airmen. Dir. Robert Markowitz. HBO, 1995.

Web Sites

Visit our Web page for links about the Tuskegee Airmen:

http://www.childsworld.com/links

NOTE TO PARENTS, TEACHERS, AND LIBRARIANS: We routinely verify our Web links to make sure they are safe, active sites—so encourage your readers to check them out!

INDEX

Airplanes, 6, 7, 13, 18–19, 22, 23
  P-40 Warhawk, 18
  P-51, 23
Allied powers, 22
Anderson, Charles Alfred, 7, 12–13
Anzio, Italy, 22
armed forces, 5–6, 7, 24, 25–26
Atlantic Ocean, 17
aviation shows, 7
Axis powers, 15, 25, 26

Casablanca, Morocco, 18
Civil Rights Act, 10
Civilian Pilot Training Act (CPTP), 9–10
Congressional Medal of Honor, 27
Custis, Lemuel, 14

Davis, Benjamin O., Jr., 12, 13, 14, 15, 18, 19, 23
Davis, Benjamin O., Sr., 12
DeBow, Charles, 14
double victory, 25, 26

England, 5
Europe, 5, 7, 17
Executive Order 9981, 26

Forsythe, Albert E., 7
France, 5

Germany, 5, 19, 22, 23

Hitler, Adolf, 5
honors
  Bronze Stars, 24
  Distinguished Flying Crosses, 24
  Purple Hearts, 24

Japanese, 15

Marshall, George, 21
military flying, 13, 19, 22, 23
Momyer, William, 19

Nazis, 5
North Africa, 17, 18–19

Pan-American Goodwill Flight, 7
Pantelleria, 19
Parrish, Noel, 13, 15, 17, 25–26
Pearl Harbor, 15
planes. See airplanes

Racism, 13, 18
Red Tails. See Tuskegee Airmen, 332nd Fighter Group
Roberts, George, 14
Roosevelt, Franklin, 15
Ross, Mac, 14

Segregation, 6–7, 9, 10, 13, 19, 25, 26
Sicily, 19
Stimson, Henry, 15, 17

Time magazine, 19
Truman, Harry S., 26
Tunisia, 19
Tuskegee Airmen
  99th Fighter Squadron, 15, 17, 18–19, 21, 22
  99th Pursuit Squadron, 7, 14–15
  100th Fighter Squadron, 15
  332nd Fighter Group, 21, 23–24
  Class 42-C, 12, 14
  combat, 17, 19, 22, 23
  impact, 7, 22, 24, 26–27
  training, 7, 9–13
Tuskegee Airmen, Inc., 27
Tuskegee Army Air Field, 7, 10, 12, 14, 15, 24
Tuskegee Institute, 7, 9–10
Tuskegee, Alabama, 7, 10

United States, 6, 7, 9, 10, 13, 15, 19, 25, 26
U.S. Air Force, 14, 19, 27
U.S. Army, 6, 12, 15, 18, 19, 21, 25
U.S. Army Air Corps, 6, 7, 10, 13, 14
U.S. Army Air Force, 14, 22, 23
U.S. Congress, 9, 27
U.S. Department of War, 7, 21
U.S. Navy, 6

West Point, 12
World War I, 5
World War II, 7, 13, 15, 19, 24, 25, 26, 27